Standing By The Stars

A Collection of Poetic Volatility

Jauni Hopesphire

BookLeaf Publishing

India | USA | UK

Dedication

For My Love <3
Never give up.

Preface

As someone with many different mental illnesses, I have found it hard to stay consistent, or motivated, in my work. This poetry compilation is a final product of my refusal to give up on myself. These poems were written across different phases of my life, and cover a multitude of emotions and mindsets. Some of these works were written when I had just become an adult - confused, conflicted, and ultimately naive. Others were written throughout my journeys with motherhood and marriage. Some catalog deaths I've endured - of those I love, as well as loss within myself; while others are focused on love and gratification. However, all of them expose different facets of my identity and my experiences. My hope for this book is to create a well-rounded examination of my life through the lens of my emotional volatility. For, as much as it has caused me to struggle... without it, I wouldn't be myself.

Acknowledgements

Firstly, I'd like to thank my ever-supportive partner, Jamee. Without him I would have been completely lost, slowly drowning alone under the ocean of my mental illnesses. He has been an absolute rock - anchoring me in place, while helping me learn how to swim.

Second, I'd like to thank my wonderfully chaotic children - they are my inspiration, motivation, and also one of the sources of my overwhelming insanity. I've grown so much through parenthood. I've learned so much about the complexities of life and love. You all have taught me so much about myself and the world, and I am forever grateful.

I'd also like to give a shoutout to my step-mother, Adrienne, for all the emotional support and understanding that she's given me over the past year or so. She has been a beacon of light during my dark days, and I have deeply appreciated each and every conversation we've had.

In that same breath, I'd like to thank my sister - Satarupa. Even though she is busier than a bee, she always has an open ear and a shoulder to cry on. She has made me feel valid through all my depressed ramblings, anger-filled rants, and spontaneous enthusiasm. She is the best sister anyone could ever have.

Lastly, I'd like to thank my great grandmother, Dolores, for always believing in me and pushing me to shoot for the stars. She knew me on a different level than most others do - she truly saw me. And she encouraged me at every turn. Though she is not with us anymore, I can still feel her near me. Watching over me. Her love and strength has kept me going.

His Eyes

His eyes - it all started with his eyes.
They playfully called to me.
It burned my soul with a sort of aching
that itched away at the back of my mind
for many months - unspoken.

It lingered inside of me;
it wouldn't leave.
Slowly it ate away at my soul
til I was nothing
but a shell of my former self.

I refused to acknowledge it,
refused to see it or accept it,
and so eventually it devoured me.

At the time I didn't realize
how badly I needed him -
not his body, or even his mind,
but his soul.

It was the only thing
that could spark a flame
inside of me.
Without it
I was empty,
cold.

Yearning without knowing
ever since I had had a taste,
but I hid it from myself.

I refused to know
what my soul had become aware of -
I buried it.
I torc it out of my chest;
ripped open my flesh and grabbed it,
strangled it,
and hid it away.

So I no longer could tell
what I truly wanted,
or needed.
I was disconnected from myself.

For all purposes of self reflection,
I was dead.

But his eyes,
they still called to me.
And the aching itch never stopped.

The Deceased

Your words twisting inside my head,
I push them away - pull at that thread,
And I'm here alone again,
Sulking inside my skin.

Somehow I always end up alone,
Break my own flesh and bone,
Terrorize my gullible mind,
And I'm left weeping inside.

Each reaction like a stab in the heart,
I pull you closer just to spit in your eye,
If only you could see I'm dying inside,
How deeply my own hands have hurt me.

Stripping off my flesh piece by piece,
Within my thoughts are eating me,
Rapid cycle of abuse and cruelty,
A single smile meaning nothing.

To my soul's end I twist and turn,
Your fingers wrapped around my urn,
These dull eyes are empty mirrors,
Slowly I'm consumed by my fears.

Vacancy

Come one, come all
Try to fill
Try to please
Try to maintain

There's a vacancy
Inside my chest
Beneath my breast
You hear no beat
For there's a vacancy

Come one, come all
It's an open, empty place
You can cover it with paint
You can fill it with your things
Bring your baggage in
Stop and stay a while
See the frozen smile
Yes, there's a vacancy

This hole inside my heart
It's tearing me apart
Please come and see
There's a vacancy

If you want a place to hide
If you want somewhere to stay
No need to push
No need to pay
It's an open door policy
Come and go as you please
Yes, there's a vacancy

Hidden

There's another me,
hidden away,
beneath this face.

Another time,
another place,
you'd see me a different way.

I'd be a me
that I'd wish to see
within my reflection.

The someone else
I hold inside
and try to hide away.

Another time,
another place,
a different face.

You'd see within
upon my eyes,
not my outer shell.

Instead of this
constructed hell,
I could open.

You could tell
that I was whole
within myself.

Not hidden away
beneath this face
inside my shell.

Because the face,
in my reflection,
would be me.

I Should

I should do more.
Two legs - four walls.
I should do more.

What can I do?
Useless hands.
Useless feet.
What can I do?
Useless brain.

I should do more.
Two legs - four walls.
I should do more.
I should.

I Withered

Below the swaying trees
near the pond of golden morning
A day came and went
as I sat kneeling.

I aged there,
within the open air.
Amongst the flowers blue
I withered.

My heart danced
amongst the stars unseen
As I held you deeply
your voice upon the wind.

Below the swaying trees
near the pond of blackened night
A day came and went
as I sat kneeling.

You died there,
within the open air.
Amongst the flowers red
I withered.

Haunted

Tempting as it is
I cannot run.
I can feel her
she's right on my tail.
She's surrounding me.

There's no end anymore.
There's no beginning.
This is it
I am here.

Time spins in circles
around me it goes.
I'm trapped within it
but I avoid the flow.

This space has become full
and it leaves me empty.
With no concept of future
I lose my control.

This cyclical reality
it haunts me.
But I cannot run
she's right on my tail.
She surrounds me.

Time Warp

Am I alive?
How long have I been here?
Days?
Months?
Years?
Time slips through my tight grasp like air.
And in a moment I have grown and grayed.
Wrinkles leave deep departure tunnels for the tears on
my face.
As I glance back at my reflection I am once again young
and beautiful –
without sorrow or regret.
Have I aged?
Am I young?
Time eludes me as my perceptions slowly change,
warping my image.
Have I changed?
Am I still the same?
How long have I been here?
I stare anxiously at the clock.

The hands almost run but for an instant they hold still.

Who am I?

I hear someone call my name and I snap back into
myself.

The faucet running wildly.

I scrutinize the clock's hands as they yell at me.

Only 5 minutes have passed but it feels like a lifetime.

I don't even know myself anymore.

I sigh, close my eyes, and try to prepare for reality.

She

She kissed me,
as the rain fell.
Her lips like rose
petals against my skin.
Her presence hanging
like thick clouds.
Her scent spread
throughout my room.
Her back arched
against the mattress.
Her body glowing
like the moon.
And as the rain fell,
she kissed me.

The Infinite Moment

Four walls – dimly lit.
Silence.
A faint breath.
The rough flicking of a match against the cement.
Fiery amber appears as the cigarette ignites.
A deep breath – a slow exhale.
The shadowy smoke rising from parted lips.

Again silence.
Silence and the light of the fire – a small orange ball
bouncing nervously with the twitching of a frantic wrist.
Anxious tapping.
Anxious and rhythmic within waiting.

Subtle pounding.
The imaginary clock pauses – waiting for affirmation.
Breathing quickens with each long second uncounted.

Louder – a couple knocks and a kick.
The hands so furious confirm all suspicions.

A muffled cough hides tensely in the corner.
Smoke releases from a coil and slithers up the wall like a
vicious snake thought through desperate hesitation.

One last knock on a door almost lost amongst the
darkness.
Then silence.

A few moments pass and the clock begins to tick away
as before.
Air escapes tightly expanded lungs with rapid precision.
Then a sigh.

Gratifying abandonment.
And an upward curling of the lips.

Freedom.

Crumbling

I can feel the absence.
I can feel the pain.
Like a shell inside a clenched fist,
I'm crumbling.
I've been crushed.

I can feel the tears,
I feel them bubbling.
The sobs building inside my throat,
My chest tight.
I want to scream!
I want to cry!
I'm suffering.

I can feel the absence.
I can feel the pain.
Like a forgotten blanket in the rain,
It is soaking up through my skin.
And I'm melting.

My body bare.
My eyes blank.
My insides festering,
Like a bad thought pestering.
My mind unraveling,
I've come undone.

And in the silent light,
My soul is left.
I can feel the absence.
I can feel the pain.
Watch me as I self destruct,
My sanity is crumbling.

The Unseen

There's an emptiness that lingers in the space you used
to fill -
An aching that my mind finds no cure for.

In-between the shapes and colors, outside of the light,
where the blank space creeps in... that's where I've come
to search.

A tree was cut down at a nearby park. There's nothing
there now but the vacancy that reminds me that it is
gone.

During silences I can hear echos of your laughter. A
bitter taste floods my memories as I think of the songs I'll
no longer hear you sing.

Your smile now just a hollow silhouette that haunts me.
That light once so full in my heart has become so
undeniably desolate.

I am left here wanting. Yearning. Trying desperately to catch any shred, or glimpse, of you that may permeate this void.

And yet, I continue to feel abandoned. Like a fawn waiting patiently for its mother to return, alone and afraid - I stay.

Hope is all I have. Hope that your figure soon appears upon the chasm with which you have left me.

A prayer that this ceaseless chill, that has come to live under my skin where your warmth used to cradle me, will fade. And that I shall be returned home to you.

Until then I am destined to lay here. Depleted. Consumed by this emptiness you have left behind.

Falling incessantly through the cracks that your absence has created. Yet vigilant to any sign that you might be near.

Moments upon moments now, I have been grasping at things that are out of my reach for they are no longer there. But you are there, aren't you? Watching me.

I feel your presence in every sadness that arises in my

chest. In the wind that caresses my face. You are all around me. Everywhere... simply unseen.

Pink Lips

Two pairs of pink lips,
wrapped around intertwining tongues.

Four hands touching,
fingers tracing skin.

Four hands grabbing,
fingers nestled in thick hair.

Eyes rolling, eyelids fluttering,
moans diving deep into open ears.

Chests rising, breasts falling,
exhales moist on the nape of the neck.

Legs coiling, toes curling,
bodies gently caressing.

Four hands playing,
fingers softly stimulating flesh.

Intertwining tongues hidden beneath
two pairs of pink lips.

The Hours

Here she is,
My daughter –
Growing.
And I'm missing it.
Wasting it.
For every smile –
I long to want.
Yearn to feel.
But I never do.

Her –
Such a gift.
Such a blessing.
And I lie here –
Empty.
An utter sense of absence –
Lingering.
A void –
Where my soul once was.
Aching –

Unable to try.

How I wish to teach,
And help her.
To give her the world.
But I am dried up –
Hollow.
I have nothing to give.
Nothing but my fleeting moments.
Nothing but a distant touch.

And yet
She has such hope.
Her eyes –
Tear through me.
So trusting.
Such love.
The need holds me here,
Holds me to her.

But how can I ever
Be enough?
Never.
Never.

Shadows of my mind
Walk along the edge.

Mere reflections of the past.
Like ghosts –
They haunt me.
Giving me hope
Laced with sorrow.

How can I ever?
When I have nothing.
Though she needs me,
A different me.
How can I?

Survived

And with her pen she tore it all down -
the only certainty she had ever known;
the ink washing away the wreckage
of her failed marriage.

With this thought she sat a while,
hands resting upon the page;
she allowed it to ruin her
and helplessly she remained.

Her mouth full of words she'd never said -
each now dripping from her tongue,
a dark puddle across the empty lines;
written boldly, "I survived."

Country Life

Mud splattered up the side of the metal,
like paint against a blank canvas,
as it sat upon four wheels that spun
like the heads of pinwheels in the spring.

The wind like music in the trees,
each leaf a single part of the melody;
with blades of grass on strings,
and the percussion of beating wings.

Breath rolled across the grass at night,
starlight twinkling in your eyes,
and we watched the heaven's dance;
a simple worldly romance.

As the earth was kissed by the morning sky
we embraced the scent of fresh flowers;
blending into the empty spaces within the land,
our mud splattered pinwheels left for hours.

Passed

Though time has passed
I still hold you
Deep within my heart
Deep within my soul

Though time has passed
I still hold you
Deep within my mind
Deep within my thoughts

Though time has passed
I still hold you
Deep within my love
Deep within my love

I still hold you
Deep within me
Though time has passed
You're still there

Caged

I sit upon this empty stage,
Looking out through my mind's own cage.
Lifeless faces stare blankly at me,
Their eyes blackened so they cannot see.
I take a bow and try to run,
Desperately I search for a glimpse of the sun.
They still just sit there patiently,
Untorn by this show's tragedy.
With a silenced voice I begin to screech,
No one notices the tears running down my cheeks.
The audience grows bored as time ticks by,
And as the curtain closes they let out a sigh.

Nothing Compares

Nothing compares to
the empty spaces
between the bare branches
of the grey winter trees.

Not the flood
of painted color
across the sky
at sunset.

Not the golden
blood of morning
spilling out
at sunrise.

Not the parade
of falling leaves
on a windy
autumn day.

Not even the
unforgettable glee
of fresh open buds
at the birth of spring.

No,
nothing compares to
the empty spaces
between the bare branches
of the grey winter trees.

When I am Old and Grey

When I am old and grey,
I'll clip branches off my tree,
And never will I worry
About the way I used to be.

When I am old and grey,
I'll sip lemonade by the sea,
And never will I worry
About the way I used to be.

When I am old and grey,
I'll lay with flowers in my hair,
And never shall I worry
For life will have taken me there.

When I am old and grey,
My eyes will lack all despair,
And never shall I worry
For life will have taken me there.

When I am old and grey,
I'll live full and free,
And never will I worry
About the way I used to be.

When I am old and grey,
I'll clip branches off my tree,
And never shall I worry –
I'll be where I'm supposed to be.

Standing by the Stars

Even if we can't stay friends,
I hope you're there in the end.
When the lights go out,
When the sun burns blue,
I'll be standing by the stars
Waiting patiently for you.

Even if our worlds are torn apart,
At the end we can have a new start.
When the sun sinks into the earth,
When the skies close around we two,
I'll be standing by the stars
Waiting patiently for you.

Even if we never come together,
We'll still be birds of a feather.
When the planets collide,
When the final moments are due,
I'll be standing by the stars
Waiting patiently for you.